PROVEN SECRETS FOR OVERCOMING PROCRASTINATION IN 3-MINUTES

ACHIEVE SUCCESS AND AVOID STRESS & MISSED DEADLINES

PATRICK BRADLEY

Text Copyright © Patrick Bradley

Legal & Disclaimer

The information contained in this book and its contents is not designed to replace or take the place of any form of medical or professional advice; and is not meant to replace the need for independent medical, financial, legal or other professional advice or services, as may be required. The content and information in this book has been provided for educational and entertainment purposes only.

The content and information contained in this book has been compiled from sources deemed reliable, and it is accurate to the best of the Author's knowledge, information, and belief. However, the Author cannot guarantee its accuracy and validity and cannot be held liable for any errors and/or omissions. Further, changes are periodically made to this book as and when needed. Where appropriate and/or necessary, you must consult a professional (including but not limited to your doctor, attorney, financial advisor or such other professional advisor) before using any of the suggested remedies, techniques, or information in this book.

Upon using the contents and information contained in this book, you agree to hold harmless the Author from and against any damages, costs, and expenses, including any legal fees potentially resulting from the application of any of the information provided by this book. This disclaimer applies to any loss, damages or injury caused by the use and application, whether directly or indirectly, of any advice or information presented, whether for breach of contract, tort, negligence, personal injury, criminal intent, or under any other cause of action.

You agree to accept all risks of using the information presented inside this book.

You agree that by continuing to read this book, where appropriate and/or necessary, you shall consult a professional (including but not limited to your doctor, attorney, or financial advisor or such other advisor as needed) before using any of the suggested remedies, techniques, or information in this book.

TABLE OF CONTENTS

INTRODUCTION

CHAPTER 1

UNDERSTANDING PROCRASTINATION TO DEAL WITH IT EFFECTIVELY

The silent killer that messes your life & kills your goals

At one point in our lives, we have said to ourselves I don't feel like doing it now, I will do it later, or It is not even the deadline yet.

We can all identify with procrastination, but none of us ever wants to admit that we are procrastinators. Instead, we end up giving justifications of why we cannot accomplish a specific task at a certain time. We embrace the habit unknowingly.

What we do not realize is that procrastination keeps robbing us of our opportunities in life and the long run it kills our goals. You might have a desire to change, improve or achieve something but you can't make up your mind about taking a step towards the right direction. For instance, you may end up missing out on a window of opportunity by failing to beat a deadline on a job application.

We can define procrastination as an act of self-sabotage, it is the fear of making a change or doing something now.

The sad part is that some of us only make the realization after years of wasted time and losing on plenty of opportunities. There is a lucky lot however that discover early in life and decide to do something about it.

The truth about procrastination - is it a habit, am I truly lazy and can you beat it?

Procrastination starts with 'I will do it later' but later turns out to be the last minute and at times even a never. It is a habit that builds up slowly without you realizing it. You begin by procrastinating the small stuff that does not seem like a big deal, but in the end, it will slip in on the stuff that matters.

Each time you decide to procrastinate a task, you reinforce the habit of procrastination. Hence it is important that we understand the top causes of procrastination and stop it before it becomes a lifelong habit.

Top causes of procrastination and how to stop them?

We may give different reasons for procrastination relating to how we feel, what we believe or the task at hand. Here are some of the top causes

Fear of Success or Failure

When we are afraid of succeeding because of what comes along with success. Others fear failure at a task, we tend to put it off and instead keep ourselves busy with other unrelated tasks to avoid the real one.

Underestimating Time Required

We at times assume that we have all the time in the world, but we forget to take into account that things do not always flow the way we want them to. It is, therefore, better to start on things early to avoid any obstacles.

Difficulty in Finding Motivation

Having the right motivation is the best way to help us accomplish a task, but at times we do not feel motivated.

We procrastinate in the name of trying to get into the right mood and find motivation but sometimes we ought to do what we feel like not doing.

Distractions

Our concentration spans are very short, and we can easily be distracted by things around us. Some may find themselves viewing a funny clip from their social media page which ends having to take them a lot of time to try and regain focus on their task.

Pressure for Perfectionism

Some people have pressure to accomplish perfect tasks due to the expectations others have of them. This kind of demand slows them down as they would try to procrastinate to come up with flawless results.

Lack of Clarity

Lack of clear goal often makes things seem difficult to achieve. It pushes people to look for paths of least resistance. We find ourselves doing that which feels simple and comfortable like watching movies or doing laundry.

Consequences of procrastination

Procrastination does more harm than good. Here are some of these consequences:

Missing on Deadlines

If you keep procrastinating the things that you are supposed to do then chances are that you will miss out on the deadlines. This habit could have serious consequences on your career, health, family, and life in general.

You need to go for that doctor's check-up before it is too late or fix issues in your family before you run out of an opportunity to do so.

Incurring Extra Expenses

Some of us receive the mail for utility bills but other than making the payments; we keep procrastinating. Before we know it our water or electricity is disconnected. We end up paying unnecessary charges to have them reconnected.

Loss of Self-Confidence

Procrastination slowly slips and takes control over your life. As a result, your reasoning becomes impaired, self-discipline and self-drive lessen. It increases the levels of failure which lowers your self-esteem and self-confidence.

Loss of Opportunities

When you have timelines, you tend to put off things up to the last minute. The pressure of the last minute does not always work well.

Undermines Career Performance

The farthest you can go in terms of your career is highly dependent on how you carry out your work. If you keep procrastinating any of the above, then you are certainly sabotaging your career.

Success stories

Procrastination Almost Robbed Me of My Future

John admits how he used to be a procrastinator. For many years, he would leave almost everything undone. In his twenties, it cost him a really good job, and that led him to acknowledge that he had a serious problem. He made efforts to try and quit which included kicking himself whenever he found himself putting things off.

He, however, realized that beating procrastination was not going to be as easy as he thought it would be. It is then that he decided to come up with a solid plan of how he was going to get out of it. He began by developing very clear and manageable goals about what he wanted to achieve such as writing his monthly work report by 2nd of every month and religiously sticking to it. Through this process, he gradually managed to regain some self-discipline and has been self-aware since then. He states that stopping procrastination requires a ton of effort, but it is achievable.

Procrastination Affected My Financial Goals

Cindy's story is no different; she started the procrastinating habit when she was in high school. She simply felt that she is the type of person that works well under pressure. While that might have worked well for her in high school, in college things were not that great. She wasn't getting all the good grades she had hoped for.

It went on into her adult life and greatly affected her financial goals. She had zero savings and was always very irresponsible with her spending. 'I keep thinking of all the years I wasted in my adult life' she says.

She decided to learn from her past experiences and mistakes and focus on what she can to move forward.

She now deliberately chooses to be responsible with her finances in every little financial choice she makes daily. She budgets for every coin and is accountable for everything, and has developed a system for her savings. 'It is not too late to make a change' are her remarks.

Stop Procrastinating and Realize Your Dreams

Robin Sharma, a known author of one of the best-selling books, 'The monk who sold his Ferrari,' is an example of what more we could achieve if we stop procrastinating.

He is from a very humble family, and life was not very smooth while he was growing up. He admits that all his life he faced critics, doubters, and disbelievers.

He worked hard in life and became a very successful lawyer, but he always felt like he wasn't living the life of his dreams. After struggling with the idea for a very long time, he finally decided to start his career as an author, and it is only then that he became more successful than he had imagined.

His decision to change in life has earned him a seat at the table with the people he considered his heroes such as Richard Branson. In addition to that, he has traveled to many countries across the continents.

Our decision to procrastinate the fear we have for the task. Robin's success story teaches us that we cannot let the fear of the unknown hold us hostage in an unhappy life. We can pursue our desires and, in the end, have the best outcomes that we hope to achieve.

CHAPTER 2

37 PROVEN AND ULTIMATE STRATEGIES TO COMPLETELY OVERCOME PROCRASTINATION WITHIN 3 MINUTES

Some experts view certain procrastination tendencies as a psychological disorder such as ADHD. While you have to accept the condition, do not be hard on yourself; you need to find effective ways to overcome it and the first step is to develop self-awareness and recognize self-worth. Do not live in denial by resisting procrastination. The only way out is to accept the challenges and develop a desire for positive changes. Here are 37 proven strategies anyone (including those with psychological disorders) could adopt to overcome procrastinations:

Start with Why: Understanding Why You Procrastinate

According to Simon Sinek, "Why" is not just a word, but a powerful concept. Knowing why you procrastinate will give you a picture of what you are dealing with at the moment. This information will help in determining the "what" and "how "of dealing with it.

We might be procrastinating because of a habit of least resistance which we create over time. Since procrastination is a habit, seek to identify the procrastination triggers. List the triggers down until you have a clear picture of the symptoms and how to maneuver around these triggers.

Start with Why. Knowing the Purpose of Your Task

You need to know why you want the outcome. Knowing why you are doing a certain task will shift your focus and make it easy to take action.

To determine the purpose of the task you have to ask yourself questions such as why do you want to read the book? Why are you writing the proposal? Why do you want to start studying?

When your "why" is clear, it will be easy for you to take action. It will set you to believe in what you are doing, which gives it meaning and the urgency it deserves. With the clarity of mind and thought, you can easily overcome procrastination.

Take enough time to determine what is required for the job in terms of knowledge, skills and tools. If you wish to chop a tree with an axe it would be better is you spend most of your time sharpening your tool.

Effective Planning

Starting your day off without knowing what to do will further increase your chances of procrastinating. Therefore, you need to plan for your day. Plan your day before leaving the office or during the night.

Most people need a plan to be productive in what they do. Come up with short-term and long-term goals to guide you in the process. Every journey with a destination has to have a road map, a plan. Devote you time to establish a clear mission statement and assign S.M.A.R.T. goals (Specific, Measurable, Achievable, Realistic and Time-Bound) for your project.

Plan on Paper

It is not enough to come up with to-do lists and rely on our memories to store them all until tomorrow. Keeping a daily journal will help you declutter your mind. Writing your thoughts and plans on your journal not only improves your memory, but it also helps you track your progress.

We all have felt how the achievement hormone, Dopamine, makes us feel when we cross out a task from our to-do list. This type of feeling will be useful to you in the future, as a memory of the reward you achieve when you finish a task. You will not get full shot of dopamine if you use apps or any other available digital forms of lists.

Chunking or Pre-Crastination

Whenever you want to make a change in your life, you will find out that you have limited power and time. If the task is complex and large, you'll need to break it into smaller chunks or parts that are doable in real timeframes.

Pre-crastination is the opposite of procrastination, which causes people to finish a task faster to get over with it. To use Pre-crastination to your advantage, you need to break large projects into small, doable tasks. These miniature tasks will promote a sense of accomplishment and bring yourself closer to your goal.

This strategy promotes taking baby steps. By doing so, you will be closer to your goal if you accomplish the baby-goals that you set for yourself. Accomplishing one big task using baby steps can become a benchmark on tackling the bigger and complex task in the future.

Don't spend your time deliberating if you can finish five pages of a book in a given time frame. Take minuscule attempts like one page first, and with time you will be doing two, four or even five pages in that timeframe. Break it down again and again until it is in easy and digestible chunks.

This strategy is important when you have a task that has large scope and not very specific in what needs to be done.

Setting Time Limits and Break

Setting time limits and breaks will help you stay focused in your work. It gives you the ability to work and play at the same time. If your task is related to writing, you can use the Tony Schwartz 90-minute intervals writing schedule with breaks in between for socializing and exercise. This strategy will double your productivity.

No matter how efficient habits you build to gain productivity, it is impossible to maintain distraction-free focus for a long term. Working on a task without breaks may lead to stress and burnout, which are key enemies of productivity. You need to schedule breaks so that you can recharge, develop new ideas and stay fresh throughout the entire day.

The 80/20 Rule, 25/5 Rule & Eisenhower Matrix

The Pareto Principle, suggests that 80% of your time accounts for 20% of work that is going to make the biggest impact. You will need to identify the 20% of your work that consumes most of your time.

This rule should help you in implementing effective planning by assigns a priority level to your tasks. Identify the key task that makes the biggest difference and completes those first leaving less time to deal with the others.

Use the 25/5 rule to write down your goals. Write down 25 goals and circle the top five important. The rule separates the list into the top five priorities and 20 less important goals. You will start working on the top five priorities and avoid the less important ones. This strategy aims to create focus and clarity in your work.

The Eisenhower Matrix is a useful tool in prioritizing work based on urgency and importance. We all agree that it is counterproductive to efficiently complete a task which should not have been done at all in the first place. You can use Dwight Eisenhower's Eisenhower Matrix, a 2 x 2 square, to identify work that you can do, plan, delegate, automate or eliminate.

Eat the Frog

As discussed earlier, 20% of your project tasks make the biggest impact on your work. We can learn from one of Mark Twain's quotes that say, "Eat a live frog first thing in the morning, and nothing worse will happen to you the rest of the day."

If the first thing that you do is eat the frog or attempt the task that has the biggest impact on your work, then you can move with satisfaction that the rest of the work will be a walk in the park. Therefore, you have to do the most important task the first thing, preferably early in the morning. Do that large and tedious assignment in the morning or read that non-fiction in the morning when you have new energy at your disposal.

Every to-do list has one or two tasks that associate to pain. These tasks could be complex, boring or against your beliefs or philosophies. Regardless of how they affect you emotionally, you need to tackles these tasks the first thing you wake up in the morning. In the morning, that's when you have

Identify the most important and challenging task on your to-do list and work on it first. By doing this, you will free up your mental energy and help you manage the rest of the day.

Early to Bed and Early to Rise

Working for long hours can be detrimental to your productivity. The brain, just like a computer CPU, needs to cool down and reset. There is a need to strike a balance between work and play, and the best way to do this is by taking breaks. Working too hard causes burnouts and anxiety, which further leads to procrastination.

Benjamin Franklin once said, "**Early to bed** and **early to rise**, makes a man healthy, wealthy, and wise." These words can if taken with great seriousness; they can be used to overcome procrastination.

Sleep plays a critical role in the human body system. When you sleep, the body starts to repair damaged cells and the mind to reset. A good night sleep restores your energy and prepares you for a productive day. It is counter-productive to force yourself to study or tackle a difficult assignment when you're tired.

Set A Reminder

A reminder can bother you until you finish your task. Set alarms that remind you of the tasks that you have to do during the day or throughout the week. The strategy will make you accountable for yourself and let you track your progress now and then.

Meditation Before Work or Study

Mediating before work or study can have a positive impact on your memory, concentration, creativity, productivity, critical thinking, problem-solving, comprehension, and reading; it reduces stress and anxiety, which means no more procrastination. You can use Concentration meditation, Walking meditation, Mantra meditation, Guided meditation or Kindness meditation.

Mediation can help you stay calm and be mindful of the unnecessary thoughts going in and out in your head. A calm and less wondering mind is more productive and can easily overcome procrastination.

Devote a few minutes of your time to develop single-minded attention: Relax and deepen your breathe to be in the moment, fully focused and concentrated.

Lock Yourself into Something

This strategy seeks to put you in desperation so that you can achieve your goal. If you wanted to start your own business, you can quit your job and let the situation guide you to your dream. Famous writers and artists are known to have locked themselves in their rooms for days to avoid any form of distraction which can hinder progress.

For this strategy to work, you must be hard to contact and find. Create your own island where you can always go when you need to focus.

Reverse-Procrastination

Reverse-procrastination lets you transfer the energy and motivation directed towards fun but time-wasting activities into your work or study. You will need to identify some of the fun activities that eat up your time and delay them. Just like changing habits with habits, in this case, you will be reversing the habit to work in the opposite direction.

Replacing Habits

Certain habits contribute towards procrastination such as negative thinking, looking for tasks with least resistance, perfectionism and among others. Replacing bad habits with good ones is the key to conquer your procrastination.

You can only master the skill of deep work if you know your working habits. Replace the bad working habits with the ones that promote productivity and overcome procrastination.

Start Small and Build Up Momentum

The most difficult part of every task is the first minutes. It is the time where your creative block and resistance form a huge wall between you and your desired outcome. The thing is, the brain has a short span of attention, that is the reason why we tend to respond positively to instant gratifications or distractions.

To enter into the flow of the brain, you need to provide it with some small bits of information relevant to your task to process that information and consequently help you get immersed in the activity.

According to research, the attention span of a typical student is 10 to 15 minutes. Therefore, if you put to work 10-15 minutes of your time in starting a project, you might accomplish more than you had expected. Take baby steps, and with no time you will be done in the specified time frame.

Focus on Result, Not Perfectionism

We can all agree that the biggest waste of time is the habit of performing things to perfection. We tend to forget that our main constraint in every task is time.

Your first goal in every task should always be to complete it. In this case, think less about perfection and make sure that you are doing the right thing. Always try to get the idea first and then follow up on details about it later.

There is no perfect time to do something meaningful. Instead of daydreaming about the result, focus on getting started. Limit the amount of information you consume to avoid confusion of thought.

Self-Imposed "Now" Deadlines

If you are a keen observer, you would have probably realized that sometimes we prefer momentary pleasures than long-term brain stimulations. It clearly shows that the proximity of the reward highly influences human motivation; the further away the reward is, the more you discount its value.

Temporal Discounting is the reason why playing a video game, browsing the internet and being on Facebook or Twitter is more rewarding than studying for your exam or finishing that report.

According to Parkinson's Law, "work expands to fit the time allotted." You will be surprised how much time it takes to when you schedule a task with less time than expected. The strategy aims to boost productivity and overcome procrastination by readjusting deadlines. You will feel the urge to complete the task when you set self-imposed deadline days or weeks in advance of the actual deadline

Keep A Healthy Body

The emotional side of procrastination relates to your health. An unhealthy person will lack the spirit and joy to work, which will hinder him or her from making any actions. It is the reason why sometimes we wake up and lack the will power to do small things such as brushing your teeth or making your bed.

Your health largely determines your productivity. All you'll have to do is to eat a balanced diet and be on the move. Always make sure that you are doing something physical. Exercising further develops your brain: the body produces hormones which regulate your mood and improves productivity.

Pomodoro Technique

Highly productive people can swear on the Pomodoro technique when it comes to time management. Francesco Cirillo suggested that work can be broken down into 25-minute sessions. It is very efficient for work and studies. You can do more and have fun in the work that you are doing.

You do not need a Pomodoro timer to work on this technique, use your timer. This strategy requires that you work for 25 min on your task without interruption. After the session is over, you need to take a rest or do something relaxing like catching your breath, grabbing a cup of tea or going for a short walk. You are recommended to take a longer break, 20 - 30 min, after every four Pomodoro sessions.

This technique is most effective in an environment that has a lot of distractions. It allows you to attend to your list of distractions after the 25 session of deep work and focus.

2 Minute Rule

With our minds craving for instant gratification, it is difficult to take the first step when we face work that requires hours to complete. Instead of focusing on completing the task, you can choose to do the task for 2 minutes. The two minutes of work will determine if you can proceed with the entire work.

If a task takes less than two minutes, don't add it to your to-do list. Complete it immediately. If a task takes more than two minutes, plan for a later time to complete the task.

Emotional Management and Intelligence

Research has shown that we often overestimate how much we can complete. We assume that we can only complete a task through ability alone, not remembering that our emotions play a bigger role in determining the momentum of our work and the extent of our concentration. Now we know that we cannot always have the same energy when we started the task.

You can incite emotion by getting yourself pumped, or terrified. Motivational talks and articles can work, for a while.

Learning from Failures

Start to learn your way through. View the task as a journey or staircase which requires you to take the first step. If you are embarking on a task that you have never experienced before, it is best to learn from failure. Trial-and-error learning will help you discover what does and doesn't work.

You have the ability to make incremental improvements in your performance. The Japanese principle of continuous improvement, kaizen, has proved this concept. To overcome procrastination you must learn from failure and move on.

Change Your Philosophy

According to Tony Robbins and Jim Rohn, a change in your philosophy can easily change your current behaviors and habit. There may be something about your private life that is affecting your professional life. For instance, your philosophy could be "do the things that make you happy," but many times when we make changes in life, we have to do activities that involve pain. Unless you change the philosophy, it will just be a barrier between ideas and action.

Learn to Say "NO"

Leaning to say "No" will help you prevent others from interfering with your work time schedules. In our bid to make others happy, we are sacrificing our time and go against our duties. For most of us, No is a word that we don't often use, maybe because we do not want to hurt the other person's feelings.

What we don't know is, our failure to say "No," when it's appropriate, steal time and delays our study or work. To stay focused on your commitments, say "No" to meaningless parties or invitations, useless conversations and anything that interrupts and steals your time from accomplishing your goals.

This strategy is always efficient in an environment where new tasks or projects keep cropping up all the time. You do not want to wind up with too many commitments with limited time. Having less to do on the table can be translated to having more time to complete important and urgent work.

Define and Optimize Your Environment

Designing and optimizing your environment keeps you free from distractions and time wasting. Keeping the environment separate will increase your focus and get you in the mood to start and complete the task. Separate your business from your pleasure and keep fixed working hours. When there is a disorder in your environment, there will be a distraction in your mind.

If your study room is in your bedroom, gym or entertainment room, then there is a high chance that your brain will not focus which leads to procrastination. Defining and optimizing your environment can also mean providing the necessary resources needed to complete the task at hand. If your wish is to run a marathon, then start by getting the right gears (shoes, clothes, etc.), get access to a gym and create time to run.

Remove Distractions

According to research, the estimated number of decisions an adult makes in a day is about 35000. These findings show that there are a lot of things that are trying to grab your attention from every direction.

To avoid being distracted, you need to block out and cut down all the stimuli that tend to derail your focus. Focus on one activity for the day and give all your attention for just 2-3 hours.

Anyone who has a deadline knows that, if not controlled, internet connection can be an enemy of production. The best control for total focus is to go offline for some time or the entire working day. Chanel all your time towards relevant work; Close all tabs and programs that can stray your focus away from the main task.

Get an Accountability Partner.

Overcoming procrastination can be challenging, especially when you can't keep yourself accountable. If that is the case, there is an option of working with a partner, which can be a friend, family member or a coach. You will need to inform your partner what you are working on at the moment and schedule a follow-up time so that you can track your progress.

Most people work best when they are under supervision. Your partner can easily call you out when you start to procrastinate. This strategy will force you to stay accountable to make sure you stick to the plan. This technique is highly useful when you are starting a business.

Identify Your Most Active Time of The Day

According to research, a normal person is most productive at around 11 am. The level of productivity decreases from 11 am to 4 pm. Identifying the time of the day when you are most productive will help overcome procrastination.

You will get most things done during your peak productivity period. It does not mean that you can't be productive during your low-productivity periods, all that you require is that you assign yourself tasks that require less energy or creativity to accomplish.

Reverse Motivation

This strategy uses a counter-intuitive approach to tackle procrastination. It involves scheduling your fun activities that relate to other people and create a fear that you will miss out on your study or work. Guarantee the fun, and this will create guilt which will force you to get back to work. This strategy will motivate you in the sense that you will remember that you need to do something about yourself.

Force Yourself into A Desperate Situation

The strategy requires that you enter into a desperate situation. For example, you can gamble against your deadline, such that you lose a substantial amount of money when you don't complete in time.

You can also put yourself in debt or out of work so that you can motivate yourself into starting your own company. This strategy creates a situation similar to someone holding a gun on your head.

Play Music

Working on a boring task may take too much time to complete. To have it livelier, you can add more fun to it. One way to make a boring task more fun is by listening to your favorite music as you work on it. Music can elevate your energy levels and keep you focused when completing boring tasks.

You will find that when you add your favorite music to a difficult task, it does keep your moods and spirits high, which is important in overcoming procrastination. It could be the reason why most people decide to run or study while listening to music.

This strategy always works when you study or work from home. According to research, nine out of ten workers increase their productivity when they listen to music. Fast music will accelerate the pace at which you are working, while slow music will make you feel calm and relaxed.

When dealing with deep work or complex writing tasks, avoid lyrical music and listen to mellow tunes. A detailed work goes well with classical music, while a task that deals with creativity blend well with instrumental music. There is a lot of different music you can choose from depending on the type of work and sound quality.

Automate Routines

Yes! Technology can be used to beat procrastination. Technology through automation seeks to make our lives more efficient and timelier. Due to advancement in technology, we can now easily automate routine tasks mostly in the business industry.

You can easily automate the things that you hate about the task that you are doing. In writing, you can choose to integrate your Microsoft Word with Grammarly to help you deal with grammar, subscribe to a plagiarism checker like Copyscape to takes care of plagiarism mistakes or automate your proofreading task with proofreading platforms.

First, you should find tasks that are repeated which can be automated. Second, search for technology or software that can efficiently automate these routine tasks. In addition to automation, you can also find the best technology that can shut off gadgets and put off notifications that act as distractors when work is in progress.

Self- Motivation

Reward yourself after every milestone when you complete a tedious task. It is important to Give yourself something; it could be an intangible reward such as a pat on the back or a more tangible reward. By doing this, you will feel good about yourself by beating procrastination. That will make it easier to achieve next time.

The best motivation you can give yourself is learning to take action. You can also use positive affirmations and mantras to start working on your task. Tell yourself that you can do it and all is well.

Delegation and Teamwork

Teamwork has always worked when the workload is unbearable. Delegation is one of the hardest things for anyone to do because it confirms that you can't handle the task on your own and this beats your pride.

Learning to give up authority and putting faith on others where appropriate will cost less and take less of your time. You can save your energy for the most important tasks when you offload routine tasks from your to-do list. This strategy is suitable where work is shared among two or more people.

Visualizing Your Deadline

Visualizing yourself finishing all of your tasks in time is one of the powerful ways to fight procrastination. You can overcome procrastination by visualization that is, seeing yourself in the future having accomplished your goal.

This strategy requires that you take some of your time as see yourself at the moment when you have completed your task. Visualize the positive feeling associated when you finish your task in time.

We tend to associate the same feeling of the person on the deadline day with the present one which is not usually the case. Fixing the picture of how you want it to look like will reward you with the achievement you want.

Find a quiet place for the visualization which should be repeated once every day. The best place and time to visualize your deadline is on your bed when you are about to sleep. This strategy works together with the law of attraction which avails what you think about every time.

Work Around People Who Are Highly Motivated

Choose your friends carefully. You can overcome Procrastination by constantly associating with highly productive people. The people you that surround you have the biggest influence over your habits and behaviors. What they do for a long period of time will be reflected on you.

What you need to do is to distinguish your friends in terms of highly productive and procrastinator. After you are done with categorizing your friends, dedicate most of your time to be with your highly productive and less of it with the procrastinator. Also focus on adding more highly productive people to your circle of friends.

Improve Your Time & Energy Management Skills

Part of overcoming procrastination is knowing how to use and recover time. In terms of recovering time, you ought to perfect your skills to be fast and efficient. If typing consumes most of your time, learn to type faster. If there are shortcuts to performing your task, learn these hacks so that you can meet your deadlines in time. If you are into coding, you should be so eloquent with the keyboard shortcuts to save up on time.

Use the time you procrastinate to learn more about the task, read book and listen to material that will guide you to fully understand your task. Use your distractors to your advantage.

Just like time, energy should also be managed since you require it to facilitate the action process. If you are exhausted it is useless to take up a task that requires high levels of energy and productivity to begin and complete. You'll just have to tackle the most intense tasks while you still have the energy.

CHAPTER 3

ADDITIONAL EXPERT BONUS TIPS TO SAVE TIME FROM DECIDING (AND PROCRASTINATING)

You ought to minimize all distractions by all means. If the internet is your problem, you'll have to disable your internet connection and turn your Mobile phone on Airplane mode during your work to maintain focus. If most of your work does not require internet, it is best if you turn off your wifi.

We tend to spend much of our time constantly monitoring our emails which not only waste our time but distract us from our important duties. To avoid distractions and unproductivity, try and set aside a small-time during coffee breaks or lunch breaks to looks through the emails. People who check email only three times a day have reported less stress and productivity in their work. If something is truly important and urgent, whoever sent the email will call you.

Write down your random thoughts on your journal or computer note pad so that you can schedule a time to search online later during the day.

If you are not expecting any information related to your task through social media or phone call, it is better that you switch them off. Avoid placing your phone on your desk when you are working on something.

Binge watching Netflix, TV series, movies, and News are massive wastes of time. The addiction to screens is a big waste of time especially when the information doesn't improve your work.

Avoid getting shots of dopamine from instant gratification caused by notifications on your phone. It has led to the habit of looking for notifications after every 5 minutes which is a big waste of time. The best solution out of this form of time wasting is deactivating notification from these social media platforms.

Differentiate between business and private life by creating different accounts. Switch off personal computer and phone accounts so that you can remain with work-related communications which contribute to your productivity.

Take heavy breakfast in the morning so that you can get the opportunity to skip lunch so that you can have more time for our work.

Before you start working, inform people (colleagues, family members, or roommates) not to disturb you for a set period. Let them know that you need to focus on what you are doing right now.

Multitask, if possible, small quick duties so that you can save more time for your high productive work. Complete small tasks immediately so that you can remain with the elephant.

Do nothing to excess. Do not overeat, overwork or take more work than you can handle. Make sure that you practice moderation in everything that you do so that you can create the perfect balance that improves productivity and overcome procrastination. In addition, spend less time on email and become more efficient in your communication.

Internet becomes a distraction when you browse aimlessly through the internet more especially during the hours that she should be working purposely to accomplish the task at hand. To avoid this, disconnect the internet from the device you are working on or use one that cannot connect to the internet to help you stay focused during the time dedicated for work.

Social media avenues such as Facebook and twitter exploits real human need to communicate and connect with others and is so addictive. You are spending countless hours checking on the timelines, updates, taking pictures and posting them in these social media platforms instead of tackling the tasks that are important at that time. Hoping from one status update to another consumes most of your time which could have been used well in your task.

Even though the workplace is the right environment to do your task, some factors fuel procrastination such as holding informal meetings discussing meaningless topics. Avoid meetings that are not in line with your work goals.

The same way we use maps to know our directions, plans can be used to lead you to your goals. Always ensure that you have a to-do list or a plan to create order and a clear picture of the work structure. Allocate more time to your high priority tasks on your plan and start working on them early in the morning.

CHAPTER 4

KEY ACTION PLANS

Understand the Nature of Your Procrastination

Before deciding on overcoming procrastination, one has to understand the trigger and indicators of this habit. In war, knowing your enemies well will prepare you on how to deal with them accordingly, this also applies to procrastination. First, know which of the various types of procrastinator you are; the cause of procrastination will determine your type.

Understand the Nature of Your Work

The type of task you want to begin working on can force you to procrastination. It is important to identify if you have handled such as task before, and if it is new to you then learn how to tackle it. You will have to give the task the meaning or urgency it deserves. If your work is too big, you need to break it down or delegate.

Application of the 37 Strategies Where Necessary

The 37 strategies can be used effectively to different types of tasks and scenarios. These strategies aim at overcoming procrastination by creating time, increasing will power, managing time, breaking down work, prioritizing work and increasing productivity.

Create More Time for Your Work

For you to overcome procrastination, there are certain tasks you must do or avoid to save more time for decision making. There are certain work distractors that you must do away with before you begin working on your task.

CONCLUSION

This guide has demonstrated that you can easily overcome procrastination by defining it and applying the most appropriate strategy. The strategies were useful to the author when writing this guide. As long as you have the time and energy to work on your project, you can easily beat procrastination. Procrastination can be a good thing to perfectionist, artists and creative arts since there are no fixed deadlines.

This Proven Secrets For Overcoming Procrastination In 3-Minutes ebook is for use by students and professionals who seek to take that necessary action towards starting and finishing a task. The 3-minute strategies will help you start a business or start studying for your exams. If you can identify the cause of your procrastination, then this book will help you avoid putting off activities that you can start now.

-- Patrick Bradley

Made in the USA
San Bernardino, CA
17 May 2019